D1125958

THE DRILL

LEARNING ABOUT TOOLS

David and Patricia Armentrout

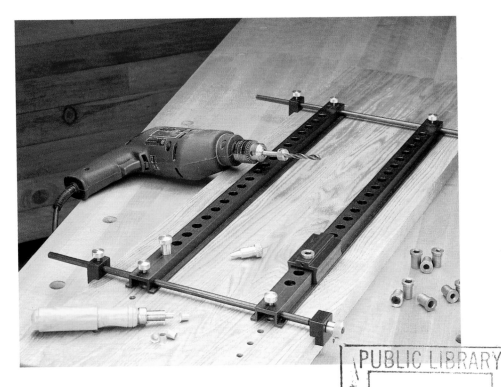

The Rourke Book Co., Inc.
Vero Beach, Florida 32964

PHOTO CREDITS
©East Coast Studios: cover, pages 12, 18, 21; © Shopsmith: title;
© Black & Decker: pages 4, 7, 10, 15; © NASA: page 13;
© Armentrout: page 17; © Fine Woodworking Magazine: page 8

Library of Congress Cataloging-in-Publication Data

Armentrout, Patricia, 1960-
   The drill / by Patricia Armentrout and David Armentrout.
      p. cm. — (Learning about tools)
   Includes index.
   ISBN 1-55916-117-5
   1. Drilling and boring machinery—Juvenile literature.
2. Electric drills—Juvenile literature. [1. Drilling and boring
machinery. 2. Electric drills. 3. Tools.]
I. Armentrout, David, 1962- . II. Title. III. Series.
TJ1263.A75 1995
621.9' 52—dc20
                               94–47277
                                 CIP
                                 AC

Printed in the USA

TABLE OF CONTENTS

THE DRILL

Hand and power drills are used to **bore** (bor), or drill, holes in almost any material. Without a drill it would be very hard to make perfectly round holes in a piece of wood or metal.

Sometimes a hole is drilled so a **fastener** (FAS-en-er), such as a screw or bolt, can be inserted in the hole.

Holes are also made to decorate a workpiece by drilling several holes to form a picture or design.

A power drill is used to bore holes before inserting wooden pegs

DRILL BITS

The drill **bit** (bit) does the actual drilling or boring. The bit is made of strong metal and comes in many shapes and sizes.

Drill bits fit into a chuck. The chuck is made to hold different size bits in place.

Some of the more common bits are the **auger** (AW-ger), used for drilling into wood, the twist drill, used to bore holes in metal, and the countersink bit, which is used to widen screw holes.

The chuck of the drill is used to hold different size drill bits

HAND POWERED DRILLS

The brace is a hand powered drill that has remained unchanged for many years. The brace has a U-shaped metal shaft that is turned around by hand to drive the bit into wood.

The hand drill is also a hand powered tool. The crank of the drill is turned around to move the gears. The gears spin the bit into wood or thin sheets of metal.

A brace is a common drill used when making furniture

DRILL USES

Over the years homeowners have become more involved in remodeling their homes. They buy tools to be used for repairs as well as home improvement projects.

One use for the drill is to bore holes in a wall. Fasteners, like screws or nails, can then be used to attach supports for a shelf.

A drill is also needed to install an overhead light or ceiling fan. A hole is drilled in the ceiling to allow the electrical wire to pass through.

Portable electric drills are used in home improvement projects

All drill bits are washed off in the factory before being sent to the store

Power drills are used to construct space ships like the shuttle Endeavour

PORTABLE ELECTRIC DRILLS

Portable (PORT-a-bul) power, or electric, drills are the tool of choice for craftsmen needing to bore holes. Electricity is supplied through a cord that enters the tool through the bottom of the handle. Cordless models use electricity stored in a battery inside the tool.

Portable drills are made in two common sizes. The smallest and least powerful drill is used to bore small and medium sized holes in wood or thin metal. Larger, more powerful drills are used for heavy-duty work.

Electric drills make it faster and easier to drill through metal and wood

ELECTRIC DRILL ATTACHMENTS

Portable electric drills can be used for more than just boring holes.

Attachments or accessories give portable drills extra uses.

Sandpaper discs attached to a drill convert it to a **rotary** (ROE-ta-ree) sander. A grinding wheel attachment can be used to sharpen scissors and knives. Buffing wheels can be used to wax a car.

Power drills can be used to shine cars when a buffing wheel attachment is used

THE DRILL PRESS

A drill press is used when an accurate, or **precise** (pree-SISE), hole is needed.

The drill press is really just a drill placed on a stand attached to a heavy table. A handle on the side of the drill is used to slide the drill up and down on the stand. Because the drill is attached to the stand, it is much easier to bore perfectly positioned holes.

Professionals use big stand-up drill presses. Home craftsmen usually own smaller bench top models.

DRILL MAINTENANCE

Hand powered drills require little maintenance, or care. Occasionally a drop of oil should be applied to moving parts. Be sure that all parts of the drill are tight and free of damage.

Electric drills should be wiped down with a clean cloth. Cords should be checked to make sure they are not frayed.

Drill bits require the most care because they receive the hardest use. Keep drill bits dry and sharp. Dull drill bits can be sharpened with an electric bit sharpener.

A drop of oil on the drill bit keeps the bit from getting too hot during use

DRILL SAFETY

When using any drill, care should be taken to keep hands and fingers away from moving drill bits. Loose clothing should not be worn, as it could become caught on moving pieces.

Never use electric drills when standing on or near a wet surface. Failure to follow this rule could cause a dangerous shock.

Always inspect the drill and drill bits for damage before use. Safety goggles should be worn to keep dust and flying **debris** (da-BREE) from injuring eyes.

Glossary

auger (AW-ger) — a boring tool

bit (bit) — a drilling or boring tool

bore (bor) — to make a hole by drilling

debris (da-BREE) — the remains of something broken, fragments

fastener (FAS-en-er) — something used to attach or hold
materials together

portable (PORT-a-bul) — easily moved or carried

precise (pree-SISE) — accurate or exact

rotary (ROE-ta-ree) — turning on an axis like a wheel

INDEX